© 2024 by Maximilian Ford

All rights reserved.

No part of this book may be reproduced, stored in a retrieval system, or transmitted in any form or by any means, electronic, mechanical, photocopying, recording, or otherwise, without the prior written permission of the author, except in the case of brief quotations embodied in critical articles and reviews.

Library of Congress Control Number: 202400145

Published by:

Elysium Publishing Group

1234 Enlightenment Lane

Springfield, IL 57801

Cover Design by: Maximilian Ford

Interior Design by: Maximilian Ford

Editing by: Alexander Voss

ADVANCED APP DEVELOPMENT WITH GPT-4 & GPT-4 MINI

Build Smart AI Chatbots and Tools

Maximilian Ford, Alexander Reed

and Ethan Cole

Praise for Advanced App Development with GPT-4 and GPT-4 Mini: Build Smart AI Chatbots and Tools

"A must-have for developers navigating the ever-evolving landscape of AI-powered applications. This book combines clarity, depth, and practicality in a way few technical books achieve."
— **Martin Fowler, Author of *Refactoring* and *Patterns of Enterprise Application Architecture***

"This book doesn't just teach you how to use GPT-4; it shows you how to master it. A definitive guide for developers looking to build reliable and scalable AI tools."
— **Andrej Karpathy, AI Researcher and Former Director of AI at Tesla**

"An outstanding resource that balances technical insight with actionable strategies. This is the kind of book that both beginners and seasoned developers will find indispensable."
— **Robert C. Martin (Uncle Bob), Author of *Clean Code* and *The Clean Coder***

"A comprehensive guide that tackles not just building with GPT-4, but also debugging, optimizing, and scaling AI applications—essential reading for modern developers."
— **Sebastian Thrun, Founder of Udacity and Lead Developer of Google's Self-Driving Car Project**

"A goldmine of practical knowledge and best practices for building AI-powered applications. Every chapter is packed with insights that make complex topics easy to understand."
— **Jeffrey Dean, Senior Fellow at Google Research**

"This book is the Swiss Army knife for AI developers—a powerful toolkit for building, optimizing, and scaling GPT-4-based applications."
— **Sam Altman, CEO of OpenAI**

"A rare blend of technical excellence and clarity. This book will not only guide you through building GPT-4 apps but also teach you to make them fast, reliable, and scalable."
— **Joel Spolsky, Founder of Stack Overflow and Trello**

"In a world flooded with AI resources, this book stands out. It's thorough, thoughtful, and deeply practical—a must-read for developers serious about AI integration."
— **Andrew Ng, Founder of Coursera and DeepLearning.AI**

"Clear, actionable, and comprehensive—this book is an essential companion for anyone working with GPT-4 technologies."
— **Yann LeCun, Chief AI Scientist at Meta and Turing Award Winner**

"An essential guide to building scalable, reliable, and efficient AI applications with GPT-4. This book sets the standard for AI development resources."
— **Fei-Fei Li, Professor at Stanford University and Co-Director of the Stanford Human-Centered AI Institute**

INTRODUCTION --- 7
    Why GPT-4 & GPT-4 Mini? --- 8
    The Future of App Development -- 11
    Setting Up Your Development Environment ------------------------------- 12
    Installing and Configuring GPT-4 & GPT-4 Mini -------------------------- 13
    Essential Tools and Libraries -- 15
    Preparing Your Workspace for Efficient Development --------------------- 17
    Common Pitfalls -- 18

BUILDING YOUR FIRST SMART AI CHATBOT WITH GPT-4 ---------------- 20

INTEGRATING GPT-4 MINI FOR LIGHTWEIGHT AI TOOLS ---------------- 29
    Use Cases for GPT-4 Mini in App Development --------------------------- 30
    Building Lightweight AI Features with GPT-4 Mini ----------------------- 33
    Common Pitfalls -- 37

ADVANCED CHATBOT FEATURES: PERSONALIZATION AND CONTEXT AWARENESS -- 38
    Enhancing Chatbots with Personalized Responses ------------------------ 40
    Creating Context-Aware Conversational Agents -------------------------- 42
    Handling Long Conversations and Context Management -------------------- 44
    Best Practices --- 45
    Common Pitfalls -- 45

BUILDING AI-POWERED CONTENT CREATION TOOLS -------------------- 46
    Leveraging GPT-4 for Content Generation ------------------------------- 48
    Developing Content Writing and Editing Tools -------------------------- 50
    Content Writing Tool --- 50

INTEGRATING EXTERNAL APIS AND DATA SOURCES FOR ENHANCED AI FUNCTIONALITY --------- 54

CONNECTING GPT-4 WITH THIRD-PARTY APIS --------- 56

BEST PRACTICES FOR API INTEGRATION --------- 58

USING WEB SCRAPING AND DATABASES IN YOUR APPLICATIONS --------- 58

REAL-TIME DATA PROCESSING AND DYNAMIC RESPONSES --------- 62

TESTING, DEBUGGING, AND OPTIMIZING GPT-4 POWERED APPS --------- 66

TECHNIQUES FOR DEBUGGING AI CHATBOTS AND TOOLS --------- 67

EXAMPLE: DEBUGGING GPT-4 API CALLS --------- 68

ENSURING SCALABILITY AND RELIABILITY --------- 70

EXAMPLE: IMPLEMENTING CACHING FOR FREQUENT QUERIES --------- 71

OPTIMIZING FOR SPEED, COST, AND USER EXPERIENCE --------- 74

INTRODUCTION

In recent years, the landscape of application development has been drastically transformed by the rise of artificial intelligence (AI). Developers are no longer limited to traditional programming techniques; instead, they have access to powerful AI models capable of revolutionizing how apps interact with users, process data, and create content. Among the most advanced tools in this field are the GPT (Generative Pretrained Transformer) models, particularly GPT-4 and its smaller, more agile counterpart, GPT-4 Mini. These models, developed by OpenAI, have ushered in a new era of smart app development, enabling the creation of highly intelligent chatbots, content generators, and other AI-powered tools that can enhance user experiences, automate tasks, and even personalize interactions.

This book, *Advanced App Development with GPT-4 & GPT-4 Mini: Build Smart AI Chatbots and Tools*, aims to provide a comprehensive guide to utilizing these powerful models to develop cutting-edge applications. Whether you're building a sophisticated chatbot for customer service, an AI tool for content creation, or even an app that integrates GPT-4's vast language capabilities into a specific domain, this book will take you through the essential steps of building, deploying, and optimizing AI-powered apps using GPT-4 and GPT-4 Mini.

Why GPT-4 & GPT-4 Mini?

The arrival of GPT-4 and GPT-4 Mini has been a game-changer in AI app development. GPT-4, the fourth iteration of OpenAI's generative model, has been trained on massive amounts of text data and is capable of understanding and generating human-like language with remarkable accuracy. It can perform complex tasks such as natural language processing (NLP), answering questions, writing articles, and even coding. GPT-4's ability to engage in meaningful conversations and solve complex problems makes it an ideal tool for developing chatbots, personal assistants, and automated systems.

On the other hand, GPT-4 Mini, a smaller version of GPT-4, is designed for applications that need a more lightweight solution. While it might not have the full-scale capabilities of GPT-4, it is still highly effective at running many of the same tasks, but at a faster speed and lower cost. This makes GPT-4 Mini a great option for developers working on mobile apps, real-time applications, or those seeking to optimize performance without compromising on quality.

This book will cover both of these models in depth, offering insights into how to leverage their unique strengths for different types of applications. The distinction between GPT-4 and GPT-4 Mini will be clearly outlined so you can choose the best model for your project, whether you need raw power or optimized performance.

What to Expect from This Book

This book is designed not only as a technical guide but also as a hands-on learning resource. Each chapter will delve deeply into specific aspects of app development with GPT-4 and GPT-4 Mini, providing you with practical skills that can be directly applied to your own projects. By the end of this book, you will have the knowledge and tools necessary to:

1. **Build Smart AI Chatbots**: Learn how to create intelligent chatbots that can engage in meaningful, context-aware conversations. You will explore the fundamentals of conversational design, chatbot architecture, and how to fine-tune your models for specific use cases.

2. **Create AI Content Tools**: Discover how to integrate GPT-4 into content creation workflows. Whether you're building writing assistants, content generators, or automated content curators, this book will show you how to harness the power of AI to streamline the content creation process.

3. **Develop Advanced AI Tools**: Go beyond simple applications and learn how to build advanced AI-powered tools that can solve real-world problems. These tools might include AI-driven analytics, automation systems, or even interactive educational apps powered by GPT-4.

4. **Optimize Performance**: Understand how to optimize your applications for speed, scalability, and cost. While AI can be computationally intensive, this book will teach you how to make the most of the resources at your disposal,

ensuring that your apps run efficiently without compromising on quality.

5. **Integrate GPT-4 & GPT-4 Mini with Other Technologies**: Learn how to integrate GPT-4 and GPT-4 Mini into existing tech stacks, connect them to APIs, use them with databases, and create real-time applications that interact with users in dynamic ways.

Who This Book Is For

This book is primarily aimed at developers with intermediate to advanced programming skills who are eager to dive into the world of AI app development. You should have a solid understanding of programming concepts and be comfortable working with modern programming languages like Python, JavaScript, or similar. While the book is accessible to developers of all backgrounds, prior experience with machine learning, artificial intelligence, or natural language processing will be beneficial.

Whether you are a seasoned developer looking to integrate AI into your apps or someone who has dabbled with AI before but is eager to learn more, this book will offer you practical insights that will enhance your development toolkit. For those who are new to GPT models, the early chapters provide clear, step-by-step guidance on how to get started, allowing you to build a solid foundation before diving into more complex topics.

The Future of App Development

The world of app development is changing rapidly, and AI is at the forefront of that change. GPT-4 and GPT-4 Mini are not just tools; they are platforms that open up new possibilities for what apps can achieve. With the ability to understand, generate, and interact with human language, AI-powered apps are becoming increasingly integral to industries ranging from healthcare and finance to entertainment and customer service.

As the demand for AI-driven applications continues to grow, the ability to build smart, efficient, and intelligent systems will become a key skill for developers. By learning how to work with GPT-4 and GPT-4 Mini, you are not only gaining the ability to create cutting-edge apps but also positioning yourself at the forefront of one of the most exciting and impactful fields in tech.

In the following chapters, we will guide you through the essential tools, techniques, and best practices for working with GPT-4 and GPT-4 Mini, empowering you to build apps that push the boundaries of what's possible. Whether you're looking to create a revolutionary chatbot, a creative AI tool, or an enterprise-level solution, this book will provide you with the knowledge and skills you need to succeed.

Setting Up Your Development Environment

When working with GPT-4 and GPT-4 Mini for advanced app development, setting up a proper development environment is critical for building, testing, and optimizing AI-powered applications. A well-configured environment not only ensures that your applications run smoothly but also helps you save time by simplifying the integration of APIs, libraries, and dependencies.

This chapter focuses on the initial steps required to set up your development environment, which includes installing and configuring GPT-4 & GPT-4 Mini, selecting the essential tools and libraries, and preparing your workspace for maximum productivity. By the end of this chapter, you'll be able to create a development environment that is both efficient and scalable for building advanced AI applications using these models.

Key Concepts

Before diving into the setup, it's essential to understand some key concepts and terminology related to GPT-4 and GPT-4 Mini:

- **GPT-4 and GPT-4 Mini**: These are language models developed by OpenAI, capable of performing various natural language processing (NLP) tasks such as text generation, summarization, translation, and even code generation. GPT-4 is a larger model with broader capabilities, while GPT-4 Mini is a more lightweight version optimized for lower resource usage.

- **API Integration**: Both GPT-4 and GPT-4 Mini are accessed via API calls. To interact with these models, developers need to set up API keys, manage authentication, and understand rate limits to ensure smooth communication with OpenAI's servers.

- **Development Environment**: This refers to the combination of software and tools developers use to write, test, and deploy their applications. For GPT-4 and GPT-4 Mini development, this environment typically includes programming languages (like Python), integrated development environments (IDEs), libraries, and cloud services.

Installing and Configuring GPT-4 & GPT-4 Mini

To work with GPT-4 and GPT-4 Mini, the first step is to install the necessary software and libraries. This section will guide you through the steps of setting up both models, with a focus on Python, the most commonly used programming language for AI development.

1. **Create an OpenAI Account** To access GPT-4 and GPT-4 Mini, you'll need an OpenAI account. Visit [OpenAI's website](#) and sign up. After signing up, you'll gain access to the OpenAI API, which you can use to interact with the models.

2. **Obtain API Keys** Once logged in, navigate to the API section in your OpenAI dashboard to generate an API key.

This key will allow you to authenticate your requests when interacting with GPT-4 and GPT-4 Mini.

Tip: Keep your API key secure. Avoid hardcoding it directly into your application. Instead, store it in environment variables or use a secure credentials manager.

3. **Install Python and Dependencies** Make sure Python is installed on your machine. GPT-4 development typically uses Python 3.7 or later. If Python is not already installed, download and install it from the official website.

Once Python is installed, you'll need to set up the necessary libraries. The main library for interacting with GPT-4 and GPT-4 Mini is openai. You can install it using pip (Python's package manager):

```bash
pip install openai
```

Additionally, for some applications, you may need libraries like `requests` for API calls, `dotenv` for environment variables, and `json` for handling data responses. Install these libraries with the following commands:

```bash
pip install requests python-dotenv
```

4. **Configure the Environment** Set up your environment to securely store your API key. This can be done by creating a .env file in your project directory, which will hold your API key as an environment variable.

14

Here's an example:

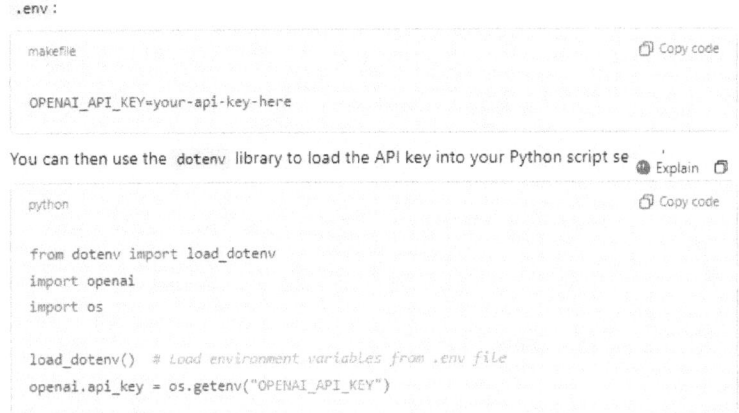

1. **Best Practice**: Never commit your .env file to version control (e.g., GitHub). Instead, use a .gitignore file to ensure it's excluded.

Essential Tools and Libraries

To work effectively with GPT-4 and GPT-4 Mini, several tools and libraries can help streamline your development process:

1. **IDEs**:

    o **PyCharm**: A powerful Python-specific IDE with features like intelligent code completion, debugging, and integrated testing.

    o **Visual Studio Code (VS Code)**: A lightweight, highly customizable IDE with support for Python, Git, and extensions for AI development.

2. **API Testing Tools**:

    o **Postman**: A popular tool for testing APIs. You can use Postman to send requests to the OpenAI API, check the responses, and troubleshoot any issues before integrating them into your app.

    o **Curl**: A command-line tool that allows you to interact with APIs from the terminal.

3. **Version Control (Git)**:

    o **Git**: Version control is essential for tracking changes, collaborating, and managing code repositories. Use Git to store and version your projects, ensuring that you can work collaboratively and revert to previous versions if necessary.

    o **GitHub** or **GitLab**: Platforms for hosting and managing Git repositories, with tools for collaboration, issue tracking, and CI/CD integration.

4. **Virtual Environments**:

    o **Virtualenv** or **Conda**: Python virtual environments are crucial for isolating project dependencies. Use them to avoid conflicts between different libraries and versions.

```bash
python -m venv gpt4env
source gpt4env/bin/activate  # On Windows: gpt4env\Scripts\activate
```

5. **Docker** (Optional): If you plan to deploy your application in a cloud or containerized environment, using Docker can help you package your app and its dependencies into a portable container.

Preparing Your Workspace for Efficient Development

A well-organized workspace ensures a smooth development process. Here are some best practices for preparing your development environment:

1. **Directory Structure**: Organize your project files into a clear directory structure. For example:

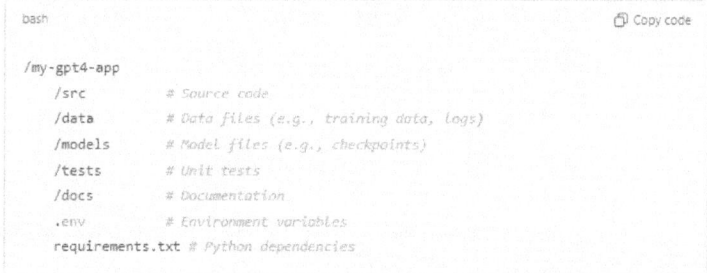

```bash
/my-gpt4-app
    /src            # Source code
    /data           # Data files (e.g., training data, logs)
    /models         # Model files (e.g., checkpoints)
    /tests          # Unit tests
    /docs           # Documentation
    .env            # Environment variables
    requirements.txt # Python dependencies
```

2. **Dependencies Management**: Use a `requirements.txt` file to list all the Python packages your project depends on. You can generate this file by running:

```bash
pip freeze > requirements.txt
```

3. **Code Linting and Formatting:** Set up a linter like **Flake8** or **Pylint** to catch potential errors in your code early. For code formatting, use **Black** or **autopep8** to ensure consistent style.

4. **Task Automation:** Use **Makefile** or **Tasks in VS Code** to automate common tasks, such as running tests or launching a local server. For example, a simple `Makefile` might look like:

```Makefile
install:
    pip install -r requirements.txt

run:
    python app.py
```

5. **Continuous Integration:** Set up **CI/CD** pipelines using services like GitHub Actions or GitLab CI to automate the testing and deployment process.

Common Pitfalls

While setting up your development environment, developers often encounter several challenges. Here are some common pitfalls to avoid:

1. **Hardcoding API Keys:** Storing API keys directly in your code can lead to security risks, especially if you push your code to a public repository. Always use environment variables to store sensitive information.

2. **Conflicting Dependencies:** Library versions can conflict with each other, leading to issues during development. This is why it's crucial to use virtual environments to isolate your project dependencies.

3. **Ignoring Rate Limits:** GPT-4 and GPT-4 Mini have usage limits. Exceeding these limits can result in API access being temporarily blocked. Be mindful of your API usage and implement rate limiting in your code to avoid hitting the API limits.

4. **Not Using a Version Control System**: Skipping version control can lead to issues when collaborating or making changes to your project. Always use Git and host your code on a platform like GitHub or GitLab.

Setting up your development environment is the first crucial step in building advanced applications using GPT-4 and GPT-4 Mini. By following the steps outlined in this chapter, you'll ensure that you have a reliable, secure, and efficient workspace for developing AI-powered apps. Now that your environment is set up, you're ready to dive into the core development of your AI-powered apps with GPT-4 and GPT-4 Mini!

BUILDING YOUR FIRST SMART AI CHATBOT WITH GPT-4

Introduction to Chatbot Development

Chatbots have become an essential part of modern applications, offering businesses and users a seamless way to interact with systems. They can automate customer service, assist with product recommendations, provide technical support, and much more. With advancements in AI, particularly with powerful language models like GPT-4, the development of intelligent, human-like chatbots has never been more accessible.

In this chapter, we will dive into building your first smart AI chatbot using GPT-4. We'll walk through the process of designing conversational flows, implementing natural language understanding (NLU), and integrating GPT-4's capabilities into a chatbot. Whether you're a beginner or an experienced developer, this chapter will equip you with the knowledge to create an advanced AI chatbot for real-world applications.

Key Concepts

Before we start building the chatbot, let's define a few key concepts and terminology that are essential to understanding how chatbots and GPT-4 work:

- **Chatbot**: A software application that simulates human-like conversations with users, either through text or voice. Chatbots can be rule-based (following predefined scripts) or

AI-driven (learning and responding based on machine learning models).

- **Natural Language Understanding (NLU)**: NLU refers to the ability of a computer to understand and process human language in a way that's meaningful. It involves recognizing the intent behind a user's query, extracting important entities (like dates, locations, or product names), and generating appropriate responses.

- **GPT-4**: A state-of-the-art language model developed by OpenAI that excels in understanding and generating human-like text. GPT-4 can be fine-tuned for various tasks, including chatbot development, and it can perform complex language-based tasks such as text generation, summarization, translation, and more.

- **Conversational Flow**: A structured representation of how a chatbot handles a conversation. It defines how the bot responds to different user inputs, ensuring smooth and engaging dialogues.

Practical Examples

Let's start by looking at a simple example of how GPT-4 can be used to build an intelligent chatbot. Below is a basic example of how to integrate GPT-4 with Python using the OpenAI API:

1. **Setting Up the Development Environment**

    o   Ensure you have Python 3.7 or later installed on your machine.

    o   Install the required libraries: openai and dotenv for securely loading the API key.

1. Setting Up the Development Environment
   - Ensure you have Python 3.7 or later installed on your machine.
   - Install the required libraries: openai and dotenv for securely loading the API key.

   ```bash
   pip install openai python-dotenv
   ```

2. Creating a .env File for API Keys Store your OpenAI API key securely by adding it to a .env file. This ensures that your key is not hardcoded into the source code.

   .env :

   ```makefile
   OPENAI_API_KEY=your-api-key-here
   ```

3. **Building a Basic Chatbot** Let's start with a Python script that interacts with GPT-4. This chatbot will take user input, send it to GPT-4, and display the AI's response.

```python
import openai
from dotenv import load_dotenv
import os

load_dotenv()  # Load API key from .env file
openai.api_key = os.getenv("OPENAI_API_KEY")

def chatbot_response(user_input):
    response = openai.Completion.create(
        engine="gpt-4",          # Use GPT-4 model
        prompt=user_input,
        max_tokens=150,          # Limit response length
        temperature=0.7,         # Controls randomness
    )
    return response.choices[0].text.strip()

if __name__ == "__main__":
    print("AI Chatbot: Hello! Ask me anything.")
    while True:
        user_input = input("You: ")
        if user_input.lower() == 'exit':
            print("AI Chatbot: Goodbye!")
            break
        print(f"AI Chatbot: {chatbot_response(user_input)}")
```

This code initializes the GPT-4 model using the OpenAI API and allows users to interact with the bot. The chatbot responds to user inputs based on GPT-4's capabilities.

4. **Sample Interaction**

```
AI Chatbot: Hello! Ask me anything.
You: What's the weather like today?
AI Chatbot: I'm sorry, I don't have access to real-time data, but I can tell you about
```

Designing Conversational Flows

Designing an effective conversational flow is one of the most important steps in building a chatbot. A conversational flow defines the sequence and logic of interactions between the user and the chatbot. For GPT-4-based chatbots, the goal is to ensure that the model responds appropriately to a wide variety of user inputs.

Here are some steps to design an effective conversational flow:

1. **Identify Key Use Cases**
   - Before creating a conversational flow, you need to determine the purpose of your chatbot. What tasks do you want it to perform? Some common use cases include customer support, personal assistants, and product recommendations.

   Example Use Case: A chatbot for an e-commerce store that assists with product recommendations, order tracking, and customer service inquiries.

2. **Define User Intents**
   - An intent is what the user wants to achieve through their interaction with the chatbot. For example, an intent could be "order tracking" or "product recommendation."

   Example Intents:
   - `TrackOrder` : The user wants to track their order status.
   - `ProductRecommendation` : The user wants to receive product suggestions.
   - `CustomerSupport` : The user needs assistance with an issue.

3. **Map Out the Flow**
   - Once you have your use cases and intents, the next step is to create a flow diagram that maps out how the conversation will progress based on different user inputs.

   Example Flow:

   ```vbnet
   User: "Where is my order?"
   Bot: "Please provide your order number."
   User: "12345"
   Bot: "Your order is on its way and should arrive within 3 days."
   ```

4. **Use GPT-4 to Handle Various Intents**
   - GPT-4's power comes from its ability to handle diverse conversational contexts. By using well-crafted prompts, you can guide GPT-4 to deliver responses based on specific user intents.

Example GPT-4 Prompt:

```python
prompt = "You are an AI assistant for an e-commerce store. The user is asking about th
```

5. **Incorporating User Feedback**
    - After users interact with the chatbot, it's important to incorporate feedback to improve the experience. You can implement follow-up questions or allow users to rate responses, which helps fine-tune the flow.

Implementing Natural Language Understanding (NLU)

Natural Language Understanding (NLU) is the process by which a chatbot interprets the user's input to understand their intent and extract meaningful information. While GPT-4 has a built-in understanding of language, it's important to use additional tools and techniques to enhance the chatbot's ability to understand and respond accurately.

1. **Intent Recognition**
    - The first step in NLU is recognizing the user's intent. With GPT-4, this can be achieved through carefully designed prompts that guide the model in interpreting the user's query.

    Example:

    ```python
    def identify_intent(user_input):
        prompt = f"Classify the intent of the following user input: '{user_input}'"
        response = openai.Completion.create(
            engine="gpt-4",
            prompt=prompt,
            max_tokens=50,
        )
        return response.choices[0].text.strip()

    user_input = "I want to track my order"
    intent = identify_intent(user_input)
    print(f"Identified Intent: {intent}")
    ```

Output:

Intent: TrackOrder

2. **Entity Recognition**

   - In addition to intent, a chatbot needs to recognize entities in user input (e.g., dates, product names, or locations). GPT-4 can extract entities based on the context of the conversation.

Example:

```python
def extract_entities(user_input):
    prompt = f"Extract the relevant entities from the following user input: '{user_input}"
    response = openai.Completion.create(
        engine="gpt-4",
        prompt=prompt,
        max_tokens=100,
    )
    return response.choices[0].text.strip()

user_input = "What are the latest iPhone models?"
entities = extract_entities(user_input)
print(f"Extracted Entities: {entities}")
```

Output:
Entities: iPhone, models

Output:

3. **Contextual Understanding**

   - GPT-4 can remember context over multiple turns, which allows it to maintain a conversation flow. This is crucial for handling multi-turn conversations, such as follow-up questions or clarifications.

Example:

```python
context = "The user is asking about their order. They previously mentioned their order"
user_input = "Has it been shipped yet?"
full_prompt = context + " " + user_input
response = openai.Completion.create(
    engine="gpt-4",
    prompt=full_prompt,
    max_tokens=100,
)
print(response.choices[0].text.strip())
```

Your order has been shipped and should arrive in the next 3 days.

Best Practices

1. **Keep the Chatbot Contextual**: Always ensure that the bot keeps track of the conversation context. This will make interactions more natural and effective.

2. **Refine Prompts Regularly**: Continuously refine the prompts and conversation flows based on user feedback to enhance the chatbot's performance.

3. **Handle Unknown Inputs**: When GPT-4 encounters an unknown input, it's essential to have a fallback response, such as asking the user for clarification.

Common Pitfalls

1. **Overloading the Model with Complex Prompts**: Complex prompts may overwhelm GPT-4, leading to irrelevant or incomplete responses. Break down the prompts into simpler, more manageable sections.

2. **Neglecting User Feedback**: Failing to collect and implement user feedback can result in a stagnant and ineffective chatbot. Regularly update the chatbot's capabilities based on feedback.

In this chapter, we explored the fundamental concepts of chatbot development, from designing conversational flows to implementing NLU with GPT-4. With the power of GPT-4, you can build conversational applications that feel genuinely human, setting the stage for more advanced AI-powered tools in your development journey.

INTEGRATING GPT-4 MINI FOR LIGHTWEIGHT AI TOOLS

As AI technology continues to advance, developers are presented with a range of tools that enable them to build more sophisticated applications. One of the most exciting developments in the world of AI is the release of GPT-4 Mini, a lightweight version of the GPT-4 model, designed to offer powerful capabilities while being optimized for performance. For app developers, GPT-4 Mini offers a unique opportunity to integrate intelligent, natural language understanding into apps without overloading system resources.

This chapter explores how you can leverage GPT-4 Mini to create lightweight AI tools in app development. From understanding use cases to building efficient, high-performance features, we'll cover how to integrate GPT-4 Mini into your app development workflow. Whether you're looking to add chatbot capabilities, automate content generation, or enhance user experience, GPT-4 Mini can be an excellent choice for creating scalable AI solutions.

Key Concepts

Before diving into practical implementations, let's first clarify some key concepts and terminology that are crucial for understanding how GPT-4 Mini can be integrated into app development.

- **GPT-4 Mini**: GPT-4 Mini is a smaller, more efficient variant of OpenAI's GPT-4 model. While it retains much of the power and flexibility of GPT-4, it is optimized for faster inference times and lower resource consumption, making it ideal for mobile and lightweight applications.

- **Natural Language Processing (NLP)**: NLP refers to the ability of a computer to understand, interpret, and generate human language. GPT-4 Mini excels at NLP tasks, allowing it to understand user queries, process language, and generate responses that are contextually relevant.

- **Lightweight AI Tools**: These are AI-driven features that are optimized for performance, requiring fewer computational resources while maintaining functional power. GPT-4 Mini is specifically designed to support such lightweight AI tools by offering a streamlined version of the full GPT-4 model.

- **Scalability**: In the context of app development, scalability refers to the ability of an app to handle an increasing number of users or data without performance degradation. GPT-4 Mini's reduced resource usage allows for better scalability when implementing AI-driven features.

Use Cases for GPT-4 Mini in App Development

GPT-4 Mini opens up a wide range of possibilities for app developers looking to incorporate advanced AI capabilities without the heavy computational cost. Here are some key use cases for GPT-4 Mini in app development:

1. **Lightweight Chatbots**

    o   One of the most common uses of GPT-4 Mini is in building lightweight chatbots that can handle a variety of user queries. GPT-4 Mini can power conversational agents that assist users with customer service inquiries, product recommendations, and more.

Example: A customer support chatbot that answers common questions like store hours, shipping policies, and product availability.

2. **Automated Content Generation**

    o   GPT-4 Mini can be used to generate content for blogs, articles, social media posts, or product descriptions. With its natural language generation capabilities, GPT-4 Mini is ideal for apps that require a high volume of content creation with minimal human intervention.

Example: An e-commerce app that generates product descriptions based on a set of input features like size, color, and material.

3. **Smart Personal Assistants**

    o   GPT-4 Mini can enhance personal assistant apps by enabling them to understand and respond to user commands with a high degree of natural language understanding. These assistants can help with tasks such as setting reminders, sending messages, or providing weather updates.

Example: A productivity app where users can query and get responses related to their schedule, tasks, and reminders.

4. **Enhanced Search Functionality**
    o GPT-4 Mini can improve search functionality by interpreting natural language queries and providing more accurate, context-aware results. It can parse user intent and provide suggestions, helping users find exactly what they need.

Example: A movie recommendation app where users can type in natural language queries like "I want to watch a romantic comedy," and the app can suggest appropriate films.

5. **Sentiment Analysis**
    o GPT-4 Mini can be used for sentiment analysis in applications that require understanding the mood or sentiment of user-generated content, such as reviews, comments, or feedback.

Example: A feedback analysis tool that evaluates customer reviews and categorizes them as positive, negative, or neutral.

Building Lightweight AI Features with GPT-4 Mini

Now that we understand some key use cases, let's dive into the practical aspects of integrating GPT-4 Mini into your app. We'll focus on building lightweight AI features and show how to leverage GPT-4 Mini's capabilities to enhance your app's functionality.

Step 1: Set Up the Development Environment

The first step is setting up your development environment for integrating GPT-4 Mini. Below is a guide on how to install the necessary libraries and configure your app to interact with GPT-4 Mini.

1. **Install Python Libraries**
   - You'll need the `openai` library to access GPT-4 Mini. Install it using `pip`:

2. **Set Up API Key**
   - You'll also need to get an API key from OpenAI. Once you have the key, you can store it in a `.env` file to keep it secure. Here's how you can set it up:

   `.env` file:

3. **Import Required Libraries**

- In your Python script, import the necessary libraries to interact with GPT-4 Mini.

```python
import openai
from dotenv import load_dotenv
import os

load_dotenv()  # Load the API key
openai.api_key = os.getenv("OPENAI_API_KEY")
```

Step 2: Building a Lightweight Chatbot

Let's walk through an example of integrating GPT-4 Mini to build a simple chatbot. This chatbot will interact with users and respond to questions based on predefined prompts.

1. **Create a Simple Chatbot Function**

    - The chatbot function will receive user input, send it to GPT-4 Mini, and return the generated response.

```python
def get_chatbot_response(user_input):
    response = openai.Completion.create(
        engine="gpt-4-mini",  # Specify GPT-4 Mini model
        prompt=user_input,
        max_tokens=150,  # Limit the response length
        temperature=0.7,  # Adjust for more natural-sounding responses
    )
    return response.choices[0].text.strip()
```

2. **Running the Chatbot**

    - The chatbot will continuously prompt the user for input and respond accordingly.

```python
if __name__ == "__main__":
    print("AI Chatbot: Hello! How can I assist you today?")
    while True:
        user_input = input("You: ")
        if user_input.lower() == 'exit':
            print("AI Chatbot: Goodbye!")
            break
        print(f"AI Chatbot: {get_chatbot_response(user_input)}")
```

Sample Output:

```vbnet
AI Chatbot: Hello! How can I assist you today?
You: What is GPT-4 Mini?
AI Chatbot: GPT-4 Mini is a lightweight version of the GPT-4 model, optimized for perf
```

Step 3: Optimizing for Performance and Scalability

One of the primary advantages of GPT-4 Mini is its ability to scale efficiently. However, it's important to design your app so that it can handle increasing demand without degrading performance.

1. **Rate Limiting and Caching**
   - When building AI-driven features, it's important to implement rate limiting to avoid hitting API call limits. Caching frequently used responses can also reduce the load on the GPT-4 Mini API and speed up responses.

2. **Asynchronous Programming**
   - To improve performance, especially for chatbot applications, consider using asynchronous programming techniques. This allows the app to handle multiple requests simultaneously without blocking the main thread.

```python
import asyncio

async def get_async_response(user_input):
    response = await openai.Completion.create(
        engine="gpt-4-mini",
        prompt=user_input,
        max_tokens=150,
        temperature=0.7,
    )
    return response.choices[0].text.strip()

# Example usage
user_input = "What is AI?"
response = asyncio.run(get_async_response(user_input))
print(response)
```

3. **Load Testing**

    o To ensure your app can scale efficiently, consider conducting load testing. This helps identify bottlenecks and allows you to optimize your code for high traffic.

Best Practices

1. **Use Clear Prompts:** When designing interactions with GPT-4 Mini, ensure that the prompts are clear and specific to avoid ambiguous responses.

2. **Limit Token Usage:** Be mindful of the number of tokens used in each API call to keep costs down and prevent excessively long responses.

3. **Monitor Performance:** Regularly monitor the performance of your AI features to ensure they are responding within an acceptable time frame and scaling efficiently.

Common Pitfalls

1. **Overloading the Model with Complex Prompts:** GPT-4 Mini may struggle with overly complex prompts. Break down tasks into smaller, more digestible prompts to ensure clarity and efficiency.

2. **Failure to Handle Edge Cases:** Ensure that your chatbot or AI tool can handle unexpected inputs and gracefully manage errors to avoid crashes or poor user experiences.

ADVANCED CHATBOT FEATURES: PERSONALIZATION AND CONTEXT AWARENESS

Chatbots have become an integral part of modern applications, offering users a quick and effective way to interact with technology. While traditional chatbots often respond based on predefined scripts or simple rule-based logic, modern AI-driven chatbots—especially those powered by models like GPT-4—are capable of providing more intelligent, dynamic, and personalized interactions. The power of AI allows for conversational agents that not only respond to direct queries but also understand user preferences, adapt to contexts, and manage long, intricate conversations.

In this chapter, we will delve into two advanced features that can significantly enhance the user experience with chatbots: **personalization** and **context awareness**. We'll explore how to design chatbots that provide personalized responses based on user interactions, as well as how to create context-aware conversational agents that remember prior exchanges and adjust responses accordingly. This chapter will provide practical guidance, real-world examples, and best practices to help you integrate these advanced features into your applications.

Key Concepts

Before we dive into the practical aspects of implementing advanced chatbot features, let's first define and explain the key concepts that are central to this chapter.

1. **Personalization in Chatbots**: Personalization refers to the ability of a chatbot to adapt its responses based on the specific preferences, history, and behaviors of the user. This involves tailoring the conversation to reflect user interests or previous interactions, creating a more engaging and relevant experience.

2. **Context Awareness in Chatbots**: Context awareness refers to a chatbot's ability to maintain and utilize the context of a conversation. This enables the chatbot to understand the user's intent not only from the current message but also in relation to the entire conversation. Context-aware chatbots can remember past interactions, track ongoing tasks, and adjust their responses accordingly.

3. **Conversation Memory**: Conversation memory is the chatbot's ability to store relevant information from past exchanges. This could include user preferences, names, frequently asked questions, or ongoing tasks. Effective conversation memory helps maintain continuity in interactions, making the chatbot feel more intelligent and responsive.

4. **Session Management**: Managing the session involves handling the flow of information within a conversation. A session represents the duration of an interaction between the user and the chatbot, and managing it involves ensuring that the chatbot can track multiple aspects of the conversation, including context and previous responses.

5. **Contextual Understanding**: Contextual understanding is the process by which a chatbot interprets the meaning of a user's input within the broader context of the conversation. This involves analyzing both the current message and the historical flow to generate accurate and relevant responses.

Enhancing Chatbots with Personalized Responses

Personalized responses are crucial for creating an engaging and user-centered experience. Instead of delivering generic replies, personalized chatbots use data about the user to craft responses that feel relevant and tailored to their needs. Let's explore how we can implement this feature.

Step 1: Collecting User Data

The first step in personalizing a chatbot is collecting relevant data about the user. This could include:

- **User Preferences**: Preferences related to the service or product offered by the chatbot (e.g., favorite genres, preferred settings, etc.).

- **User History**: Past interactions that can help understand user behavior, needs, and intent.

- **Profile Information**: Details such as the user's name, age, location, or specific needs.

Example: If you're developing an e-commerce chatbot, you may store information about the user's past purchases, product preferences, or browsing history to suggest relevant items.

Step 2: Storing and Accessing User Data

To maintain personalized interactions, you need a reliable way to store and retrieve user data. A simple method is to use a database or a key-value store like Redis to save information across sessions. This data should be linked to the user's unique ID.

```python
import json
import openai
import sqlite3

# Database setup
conn = sqlite3.connect('chatbot.db')
cursor = conn.cursor()
cursor.execute('''CREATE TABLE IF NOT EXISTS user_data (user_id TEXT, data TEXT)''')

def store_user_data(user_id, data):
    cursor.execute('INSERT OR REPLACE INTO user_data (user_id, data) VALUES (?, ?)', (user_id, data))
    conn.commit()

def get_user_data(user_id):
    cursor.execute('SELECT data FROM user_data WHERE user_id = ?', (user_id,))
    result = cursor.fetchone()
    return json.loads(result[0]) if result else {}

# Example of storing user data
user_id = "user123"
user_data = {"name": "John", "preferences": ["electronics", "gaming"]}
store_user_data(user_id, user_data)
```

Step 3: Personalizing the Chatbot Responses

Once you have user data, you can use it to personalize the chatbot's responses. A chatbot powered by GPT-4 can take this data and inject it into the prompts sent to the model.

```python
def personalize_response(user_input, user_id):
    # Retrieve user data
    user_data = get_user_data(user_id)
    name = user_data.get("name", "User")

    # Prepare personalized prompt
    prompt = f"Hello {name}, how can I assist you today? You have previously shown interes

    # Generate a response with GPT-4 Mini
    response = openai.Completion.create(
        engine="gpt-4-mini",
        prompt=prompt + " " + user_input,
        max_tokens=150,
        temperature=0.7,
    )

    return response.choices[0].text.strip()

# Example of personalized chatbot interaction
user_input = "What are the latest gadgets?"
response = personalize_response(user_input, user_id)
print(response)
```

In this example, the chatbot tailors its greeting and the conversation context based on the user's preferences and previous interactions.

Creating Context-Aware Conversational Agents

Context awareness is critical for chatbots that handle complex, ongoing conversations. A context-aware chatbot can provide better responses by interpreting the meaning of a message in light of the entire conversation history.

Step 1: Maintaining Conversation Context

To enable context awareness, the chatbot needs to track the conversation flow. This can be done by maintaining a history of interactions, either locally or in a session store.

```python
# A simple structure to store conversation history
class ConversationHistory:
    def __init__(self):
        self.history = []

    def add_message(self, user_input, bot_response):
        self.history.append({"user": user_input, "bot": bot_response})

    def get_context(self):
        # Combine the history into a single string for context
        return "\n".join([f"User: {msg['user']}\nBot: {msg['bot']}" for msg in self.histor

# Example of context management
conversation = ConversationHistory()
conversation.add_message("What is AI?", "AI is the simulation of human intelligence in mac
conversation.add_message("What is machine learning?", "Machine learning is a subset of AI

# Get the entire conversation context
context = conversation.get_context()
print(context)
```

Step 2: Generating Context-Aware Responses

Once the conversation history is tracked, you can include this context in the chatbot's prompts to make responses more relevant and informed by prior messages.

```python
def get_context_aware_response(user_input, conversation_history):
    context = conversation_history.get_context()

    # Send the full context along with the user's current input to GPT-4
    prompt = context + f"\nUser: {user_input}\nBot:"

    response = openai.Completion.create(
        engine="gpt-4-mini",
        prompt=prompt,
        max_tokens=150,
        temperature=0.7,
    )

    bot_response = response.choices[0].text.strip()
    conversation_history.add_message(user_input, bot_response)

    return bot_response

# Example of a context-aware chatbot interaction
user_input = "What is deep learning?"
response = get_context_aware_response(user_input, conversation)
print(response)
```

By using the conversation history as part of the prompt, the chatbot can generate responses that take into account the entire conversation, making it feel more coherent and contextually appropriate.

Handling Long Conversations and Context Management

Long conversations present unique challenges. As the conversation grows, the context becomes larger, which may impact performance. Efficient context management becomes critical for maintaining chatbot responsiveness.

Step 1: Limiting Context Length

One strategy is to limit the number of messages included in the context. Instead of using the entire conversation, you can keep only the most recent messages or prioritize critical exchanges.

```python
def get_trimmed_context(conversation_history, max_length=5):
    # Limit the history to the most recent `max_length` messages
    return "\n".join([f"User: {msg['user']}\nBot: {msg['bot']}" for msg in conversation_hi

# Example of trimming the context
short_context = get_trimmed_context(conversation, max_length=3)
print(short_context)
```

Step 2: Session Management

For long-running conversations, it's also important to manage user sessions. You can store the context in a session object, database, or in-memory cache to maintain continuity across multiple interactions.

Best Practices

1. **Balance Personalization with Privacy**: While personalization is important, make sure you're handling user data responsibly and in compliance with privacy laws like GDPR. Avoid storing sensitive data unless absolutely necessary.

2. **Context Management**: Limit the amount of conversation history you store to improve performance. Only store key information that impacts the current interaction.

3. **User Feedback**: Regularly prompt users to confirm or update their preferences to ensure the chatbot remains relevant.

Common Pitfalls

1. **Overloading the Context**: Storing too much conversation history can slow down performance. Always consider trimming older messages that are no longer relevant.

2. **Ignoring Edge Cases**: Sometimes, users might give ambiguous or unrelated responses. Ensure your chatbot is capable of handling such cases gracefully.

3. **Privacy Concerns**: Storing too much personal information can lead to privacy issues. Always inform users about the data you're storing and give them control over their data.

BUILDING AI-POWERED CONTENT CREATION TOOLS

In the fast-evolving world of application development, artificial intelligence (AI) has revolutionized how we approach content creation. AI-powered tools can generate, edit, and optimize content with remarkable speed and accuracy, helping businesses, developers, and content creators alike. One of the most powerful tools in this field is GPT-4, a state-of-the-art language model by OpenAI, which can generate human-like text based on a variety of prompts. By leveraging GPT-4, developers can create robust content generation and editing tools that enhance creativity and streamline workflows.

This chapter will guide you through the process of building AI-powered content creation tools using GPT-4. We will explore how to integrate GPT-4 for content generation, develop content writing and editing tools, and apply the model for creative AI applications. With practical examples, step-by-step instructions, and best practices, you'll learn how to build applications that leverage AI for dynamic and scalable content creation.

Key Concepts

Before diving into the practical steps, let's define and explain some key concepts related to AI-powered content creation.

1. **Content Generation**: Content generation refers to the process of automatically creating written material—such as articles, blogs, product descriptions, or social media posts—

using AI tools. GPT-4 excels in content generation by analyzing user prompts and creating coherent, contextually relevant text.

2. **Natural Language Processing (NLP)**: NLP is a field of AI focused on the interaction between computers and human languages. It encompasses tasks such as text generation, translation, summarization, and sentiment analysis. GPT-4 is an NLP model that generates human-like text based on patterns it has learned from vast amounts of text data.

3. **Creative AI Applications**: Creative AI applications go beyond traditional content creation by generating creative outputs such as poetry, stories, artwork, and even music. GPT-4 can be leveraged in these applications to generate ideas, refine drafts, or assist in brainstorming.

4. **Content Editing Tools**: These are AI-powered tools that assist with refining and improving written content. Editing tools can suggest grammar corrections, rephrase sentences for clarity, optimize tone, and more. GPT-4 can help enhance the content by providing suggestions for improvements in real-time.

5. **Prompt Engineering**: Prompt engineering is the process of crafting specific inputs (prompts) for AI models like GPT-4 in order to generate desired outputs. The quality of

the generated content depends heavily on how well the prompt is designed.

Leveraging GPT-4 for Content Generation

GPT-4's ability to generate text makes it ideal for a variety of content creation applications. Let's begin by exploring how to use GPT-4 to generate content automatically.

Step 1: Setting Up the Environment

To get started, you'll need to set up an environment that allows you to interact with GPT-4. This typically involves:

- **API Access**: Obtain access to OpenAI's API by signing up on their website and generating an API key.

- **Python Setup**: Ensure that you have Python installed along with the openai package, which allows you to interact with the GPT-4 model.

```bash
pip install openai
```

Once you have access to the API, you can set up the configuration to interact with GPT-4.

Step 2: Making Your First API Call

Let's write a simple Python function that connects to the OpenAI API and generates content based on a prompt. In this case, we'll create an example that generates a blog post introduction.

```python
import openai

# Set up the API key
openai.api_key = "YOUR_API_KEY"

def generate_blog_post_intro(topic):
    prompt = f"Write a blog post introduction about {topic}."
    response = openai.Completion.create(
        engine="gpt-4",
        prompt=prompt,
        max_tokens=200,
        temperature=0.7
    )
    return response.choices[0].text.strip()

# Example usage
topic = "the future of AI in healthcare"
intro = generate_blog_post_intro(topic)
print(intro)
```

In this example, we've set up a basic function that takes a topic as input and generates a blog post introduction using GPT-4. The `temperature` parameter controls the randomness of the output, and `max_tokens` limits the length of the generated text.

Step 3: Customizing Content Generation

You can further customize the content generation process by adjusting the prompt to suit specific needs, such as creating product descriptions, social media posts, or marketing copy. Here's how you can extend the code to generate a product description:

```python
def generate_product_description(product_name, features):
    prompt = f"Write a product description for {product_name}. Include the following features"
    response = openai.Completion.create(
        engine="gpt-4",
        prompt=prompt,
        max_tokens=150,
        temperature=0.7
    )
    return response.choices[0].text.strip()

# Example usage
product_name = "Wireless Noise-Canceling Headphones"
features = ["Bluetooth connectivity", "20 hours of battery life", "comfortable ear cushion
description = generate_product_description(product_name, features)
print(description)
```

By adjusting the prompt, you can generate content that meets your specific requirements for various use cases.

Developing Content Writing and Editing Tools

AI-powered content writing and editing tools can improve productivity and assist writers in generating high-quality content with minimal effort. Let's look at how we can build a content writing tool and an editing tool using GPT-4.

Content Writing Tool

A content writing tool can help generate drafts, expand on ideas, or assist with writer's block. You can create a simple tool that generates multiple paragraphs on a given topic:

```python
def generate_article_body(topic):
    prompt = f"Write a detailed article about {topic}. Include at least 3 paragraphs with
    response = openai.Completion.create(
        engine="gpt-4",
        prompt=prompt,
        max_tokens=500,
        temperature=0.7
    )

    return response.choices[0].text.strip()

# Example usage
article_body = generate_article_body("how AI is transforming the education sector")
print(article_body)
```

This function generates a detailed article body with subheadings based on the provided topic. Writers can use this as a draft, and then refine or expand it further.

Content Editing Tool

For content editing, GPT-4 can help with grammar checks, rephrasing sentences, and improving readability. Here's an example of using GPT-4 for sentence rephrasing:

```python
def rephrase_sentence(sentence):
    prompt = f"Rephrase the following sentence to make it clearer: {sentence}"
    response = openai.Completion.create(
        engine="gpt-4",
        prompt=prompt,
        max_tokens=100,
        temperature=0.7
    )
    return response.choices[0].text.strip()

# Example usage
sentence = "The project was done on a very tight schedule, and it was challenging to compl
rephrased_sentence = rephrase_sentence(sentence)
print(rephrased_sentence)
```

This function takes a sentence and rephrases it to make it more concise and readable. Developers can build more advanced editing tools by combining features like grammar correction, tone adjustment, and word choice suggestions.

Integrating GPT-4 for Creative AI Applications

Creative AI applications go beyond standard content creation by generating highly creative outputs such as poetry, stories, or even scriptwriting. Let's explore how GPT-4 can be used to enhance creativity.

Step 1: Generating Creative Writing

GPT-4 excels at creative writing tasks. For example, you can use it to generate a short story based on a given prompt:

51

```python
def generate_short_story(prompt):
    response = openai.Completion.create(
        engine="gpt-4",
        prompt=prompt,
        max_tokens=500,
        temperature=0.8
    )
    return response.choices[0].text.strip()

# Example usage
story_prompt = "Write a short story about a detective solving a mysterious case in a futur
story = generate_short_story(story_prompt)
print(story)
```

In this case, GPT-4 generates a creative narrative based on the prompt, helping authors and scriptwriters brainstorm or overcome writer's block.

Step 2: Using GPT-4 for Poetry Generation

GPT-4 can also be used to generate poetry by adjusting the prompt to include stylistic elements like rhyme schemes or poetic structures. For example:

```python
def generate_poetry(theme):
    prompt = f"Write a poem about {theme}. The poem should rhyme and have four stanzas."
    response = openai.Completion.create(
        engine="gpt-4",
        prompt=prompt,
        max_tokens=150,
        temperature=0.9
    )
    return response.choices[0].text.strip()

# Example usage
poem = generate_poetry("love and loss")
print(poem)
```

This function creates a short poem on a given theme, showcasing the creative potential of GPT-4.

Best Practices

1. **Refining Prompts**: The quality of the generated content depends heavily on the prompt. Refine and experiment with different prompt structures to achieve the best results.

2. **Fine-Tuning Models**: Consider fine-tuning the GPT-4 model for your specific domain. This can help improve accuracy and relevance for niche topics.

3. **Incorporate User Feedback**: Always consider user feedback when developing content tools to ensure the outputs are useful and of high quality.

4. **Limit Token Usage**: Be mindful of the token limits when generating long-form content. Break large pieces of content into smaller sections to optimize performance.

Common Pitfalls

1. **Overreliance on AI**: While AI is powerful, always review the generated content for quality, accuracy, and relevance. GPT-4 might produce text that sounds plausible but is factually incorrect.

2. **Too Vague Prompts**: Avoid vague prompts that result in generic or irrelevant content. Be specific in your instructions to GPT-4 to ensure high-quality outputs.

3. **Performance and Cost**: Generating large amounts of content can be resource-intensive. Monitor API usage to prevent excessive costs.

INTEGRATING EXTERNAL APIS AND DATA SOURCES FOR ENHANCED AI FUNCTIONALITY

In the age of intelligent applications, integrating external APIs and data sources into your AI-powered systems is crucial for providing dynamic, real-time, and highly personalized experiences. While GPT-4 is an incredibly powerful tool for generating text, it can be further enhanced by incorporating external data from third-party APIs, databases, and web scraping. By combining GPT-4's capabilities with external data, developers can create more robust and contextually aware applications.

This chapter will guide you through the process of integrating GPT-4 with third-party APIs, using web scraping to collect data, and incorporating real-time data processing into your applications. With practical examples and step-by-step instructions, you will learn how to build applications that are capable of pulling data from multiple sources to respond intelligently to user queries.

Key Concepts

Before diving into practical applications, let's break down some essential concepts and terminology related to integrating external APIs and data sources with AI models like GPT-4.

1. **Third-Party APIs**: These are external services that offer specific functionalities, such as weather data, financial information, or social media insights. Integrating these APIs

into your application allows you to augment GPT-4's functionality by providing it with up-to-date, external data.

2. **Web Scraping**: Web scraping is the process of extracting data from websites. In the context of AI applications, web scraping can be used to collect publicly available data, such as product prices, news articles, or even user reviews, which can then be processed by GPT-4 to generate more informed responses.

3. **Databases**: A database stores structured data that can be queried and retrieved. By integrating GPT-4 with databases, you can allow the AI model to fetch historical or user-specific data to generate responses based on past interactions or custom datasets.

4. **Real-Time Data Processing**: Real-time data processing involves collecting and analyzing data as it is generated, without delays. This is essential for applications like live chatbots or financial analysis tools, where the AI needs to react instantly to changes in data.

5. **Dynamic Responses**: These are responses generated by an AI model that change based on the latest data, user input, or other real-time factors. Integrating external APIs or databases allows the AI to provide answers that are always up to date and contextually relevant.

Connecting GPT-4 with Third-Party APIs

Integrating third-party APIs into GPT-4-powered applications is one of the most straightforward ways to expand the functionality of your system. These APIs can provide real-time data, perform specialized tasks, or even interface with other services like payment systems or social media platforms.

Step 1: Setting Up API Access

Before you can integrate an external API, you need to obtain an API key or token. Typically, this requires signing up on the service provider's platform, after which you'll be able to generate your unique API key.

Once you have your API key, you can begin integrating it into your application. Here, we'll demonstrate how to connect GPT-4 with a weather API to provide users with personalized weather information.

Example: Integrating GPT-4 with a Weather API

Let's use OpenWeatherMap's API to fetch weather data. We will integrate it with GPT-4 to allow users to ask about the weather in a specific location, and the AI will respond with the current weather forecast.

```python
import openai
import requests

# Set up your OpenAI API key
openai.api_key = "YOUR_OPENAI_API_KEY"

# Set up your OpenWeatherMap API key
weather_api_key = "YOUR_WEATHER_API_KEY"
weather_url = "http://api.openweathermap.org/data/2.5/weather"

def get_weather(city):
    params = {
        'q': city,
        'appid': weather_api_key,
        'units': 'metric'
    }
    response = requests.get(weather_url, params=params)
    data = response.json()

    if data['cod'] == 200:
        temp = data['main']['temp']
        description = data['weather'][0]['description']
        return f"The current temperature in {city} is {temp}°C with {description}."
    else:
        return "Sorry, I couldn't retrieve the weather information."

def generate_weather_response(city):
    weather_info = get_weather(city)
    prompt = f"The user wants to know about the weather in {city}. Provide a friendly and

    response = openai.Completion.create(
        engine="gpt-4",
        prompt=prompt,
        max_tokens=150,
        temperature=0.7
    )

    return response.choices[0].text.strip()

# Example usage
city = "London"
response = generate_weather_response(city)
print(response)
```

Explanation:

- We first retrieve weather data from the OpenWeatherMap API based on the user's city input.

- We then integrate the weather data into GPT-4's prompt, allowing it to provide a natural language response.

- The weather information serves as dynamic context for GPT-4 to generate relevant responses.

Best Practices for API Integration

- **Error Handling**: Always implement error handling for situations where the API is unavailable or returns an error.

- **Rate Limiting**: Many APIs have rate limits. Ensure your application handles these limits gracefully to avoid disruptions.

- **API Caching**: For frequently requested data (e.g., weather or stock prices), consider caching responses to reduce API calls and improve performance.

Using Web Scraping and Databases in Your Applications

While APIs provide structured data from external sources, web scraping allows you to gather data directly from websites. This can be useful when you need information that isn't available through a formal API, or when the data is in a free-to-access form.

Step 1: Web Scraping with Python

To demonstrate web scraping, let's use BeautifulSoup and requests to scrape a website and retrieve specific data. Here, we will scrape headlines from a news website and provide summaries using GPT-4

```python
import requests
from bs4 import BeautifulSoup
import openai

openai.api_key = "YOUR_OPENAI_API_KEY"

def scrape_news():
    url = "https://www.bbc.com/news"
    response = requests.get(url)
    soup = BeautifulSoup(response.text, 'html.parser')

    headlines = []
    for headline in soup.find_all('h3'):
        headlines.append(headline.get_text())

    return headlines[:5]

def summarize_news():
    headlines = scrape_news()
    prompt = "Here are the top news headlines. Summarize each one in one sentence:\n"
    prompt += "\n".join([f"{i+1}. {headline}" for i, headline in enumerate(headlines)])

    response = openai.Completion.create(
        engine="gpt-4",
        prompt=prompt,
        max_tokens=250,
        temperature=0.7
    )

    return response.choices[0].text.strip()

# Example usage
summary = summarize_news()
print(summary)
```

Explanation:

- We scrape the top headlines from the BBC News website using BeautifulSoup and requests.

- We send these headlines to GPT-4 to generate concise summaries for each headline.

Best Practices for Web Scraping:

- **Respect Robots.txt**: Always check a website's robots.txt file to ensure you're not violating any scraping rules.

- **Limit Requests**: To avoid overwhelming servers, limit your requests and include delays between them.

- **Legal Compliance**: Be aware of copyright and data usage laws when scraping content from websites.

Step 2: Using Databases for Data Storage

Databases are crucial for storing and retrieving large amounts of structured data. Integrating GPT-4 with databases allows you to create applications that can pull data based on user input or previous interactions.

Let's integrate GPT-4 with a simple SQLite database to retrieve user-specific information and provide personalized responses.

```python
import sqlite3
import openai

# Set up OpenAI API Key
openai.api_key = "YOUR_OPENAI_API_KEY"

# Initialize SQLite database
conn = sqlite3.connect('user_data.db')
cursor = conn.cursor()

# Create table if it doesn't exist
cursor.execute('''CREATE TABLE IF NOT EXISTS users
                (id INTEGER PRIMARY KEY, name TEXT, favorite_color TEXT)''')

# Insert a sample user
cursor.execute("INSERT INTO users (name, favorite_color) VALUES ('Alice', 'blue')")
conn.commit()

def get_user_data(user_id):
    cursor.execute("SELECT * FROM users WHERE id=?", (user_id,))
    return cursor.fetchone()

def generate_personalized_response(user_id):
    user_data = get_user_data(user_id)
    if user_data:
        name, favorite_color = user_data[1], user_data[2]
        prompt = f"Generate a friendly response for {name} who loves the color
        response = openai.Completion.create(
            engine="gpt-4",
            prompt=prompt,
            max_tokens=100,
            temperature=0.7
        )
        return response.choices[0].text.strip()
    else:
        return "User not found."

# Example usage
user_id = 1
response = generate_personalized_response(user_id)
print(response)
```

Explanation:

- We store user data, such as name and favorite color, in an SQLite database.
- GPT-4 generates a personalized response based on the data retrieved from the database.

Best Practices for Database Integration:

- **Use Parameterized Queries**: To avoid SQL injection attacks, always use parameterized queries.
- **Optimize Queries**: Ensure that queries are optimized for performance, especially if you're dealing with large datasets.
- **Backup Data**: Regularly back up the database to avoid data loss.

Real-Time Data Processing and Dynamic Responses

In many applications, you need to process real-time data and generate dynamic responses based on that data. This is especially useful for applications such as live chatbots, stock tracking systems, or social media monitoring tools.

Example: Real-Time Stock Price Querying

Let's use the Alpha Vantage API to retrieve real-time stock prices and integrate it with GPT-4 to provide personalized investment advice.

```python
import requests
import openai

openai.api_key = "YOUR_OPENAI_API_KEY"

# Alpha Vantage API key and endpoint
stock_api_key = "YOUR_ALPHA_VANTAGE_API_KEY"
stock_url = "https://www.alphavantage.co/query"

def get_stock_price(symbol):
    params = {
        'function': 'TIME_SERIES_INTRADAY',
        'symbol': symbol,
        'interval': '5min',
        'apikey': stock_api_key
    }
    response = requests.get(stock_url, params=params)
    data = response.json()

    if 'Time Series (5min)' in data:
        latest_time = list(data['Time Series (5min)'].keys())[0]
        latest_data = data['Time Series (5min)'][latest_time]
        price = latest_data['4. close']
        return price
    else:
        return "Could not fetch stock data."

def generate_stock_advice(symbol):
    price = get_stock_price(symbol)
    prompt = f"The user asked for the stock price of {symbol}."

    response = openai.Completion.create(
        engine="gpt-4",
        prompt=prompt,
        max_tokens=150,
        temperature=0.7
    )

    return response.choices[0].text.strip()

# Example usage
stock_symbol = "AAPL"
advice = generate_stock_advice(stock_symbol)
print(advice)
```

Explanation:

- We retrieve real-time stock prices using the Alpha Vantage API.
- GPT-4 provides dynamic investment advice based on the latest stock price.

Best Practices for Real-Time Data:

- **Handle Latency**: When working with real-time data, ensure your application can handle slight delays due to API calls or data processing.
- **Ensure Data Accuracy**: Real-time systems depend on accurate data. Validate and clean incoming data before processing it.
- **Update Responses Quickly**: For real-time interactions, ensure the AI's responses are generated quickly to provide users with timely information.

By integrating third-party APIs, web scraping techniques, and databases into your GPT-4-powered applications, you can create dynamic, intelligent systems that provide real-time responses based on up-to-date information. Through careful setup and optimization, you can ensure that your applications run efficiently and scale as needed.

Key takeaways:

- APIs, web scraping, and databases enable GPT-4 to access external data sources for more personalized, contextually relevant responses.

- Real-time data processing enhances the interactivity and responsiveness of AI systems.

- Following best practices for API integration, web scraping, and database management ensures reliable and efficient AI functionality.

As you continue to build and optimize your AI applications, don't hesitate to experiment with different data sources and integration methods to meet your specific needs. The possibilities are limitless!

Testing, Debugging, and Optimizing GPT-4 Powered Apps

Introduction

Developing GPT-4-powered applications involves more than just writing code to make an API call or integrate machine learning models. Once the application is built, it's essential to rigorously test, debug, and optimize it to ensure high performance, reliability, and scalability. This chapter delves into the techniques and best practices for debugging AI chatbots and tools, ensuring that your application can scale efficiently, and optimizing it for speed, cost, and user experience.

As GPT-4-based applications become more advanced, developers face new challenges that require thoughtful debugging and optimization strategies. AI systems often have intricate, dynamic behaviors, which means that typical debugging tools and approaches may need to be adapted. This chapter will help you understand the key concepts of debugging AI-powered apps, offer practical examples, and outline methods for optimizing applications for speed, cost, and user experience.

Key Concepts

Before diving into specific techniques, let's define a few key terms and concepts that are critical for debugging and optimizing AI-driven applications:

1. **Debugging**: The process of identifying and fixing errors or bugs in your code. Debugging is crucial in ensuring that

your GPT-4 application performs as expected and does not crash or behave unpredictably.

2. **Scalability**: Refers to the capability of an application to handle increasing loads or traffic without performance degradation. Scalability is especially important for AI applications that might experience variable usage patterns.

3. **Reliability**: The ability of your application to perform its intended functions consistently, without failure, over time. A reliable application can handle edge cases, exceptions, and unexpected inputs gracefully.

4. **Optimization**: The process of making your application faster, more efficient, and more cost-effective. In the context of GPT-4-powered applications, optimization involves reducing processing time, minimizing API call costs, and improving the user experience.

5. **User Experience (UX)**: The overall experience a user has when interacting with your application, including ease of use, speed, and how responsive the AI is to user queries. A good user experience is critical to the success of AI chatbots and other conversational tools.

Techniques for Debugging AI Chatbots and Tools

AI systems, including chatbots powered by GPT-4, can exhibit unpredictable behavior due to their reliance on complex machine learning models. Debugging such systems requires a mix of traditional software debugging techniques and specialized approaches for AI-specific issues.

Step 1: Identify the Source of the Issue

When debugging GPT-4-powered applications, start by identifying where the issue originates. Common areas that may need debugging include:

- **API Integration Issues**: The application may be failing to interact with the GPT-4 API due to incorrect API keys, incorrect endpoint configurations, or rate-limiting issues.

- **Prompt Engineering**: If the model's responses are inaccurate or irrelevant, this could be due to the prompt being poorly designed.

- **Data Issues**: GPT-4's performance is highly dependent on the quality of data fed into it. If your chatbot's responses are nonsensical or irrelevant, the issue might lie in the data sources being used.

Example: Debugging GPT-4 API Calls

Let's assume you have an AI chatbot that uses GPT-4 to respond to user queries. If the bot is returning erroneous responses, you need to verify the API call setup. Below is an example of how you might debug the API call.

```python
import openai
import logging

# Set up OpenAI API key
openai.api_key = 'YOUR_OPENAI_API_KEY'

# Enable logging
logging.basicConfig(level=logging.DEBUG)

def debug_api_call(prompt):
    try:
        logging.debug(f"Sending prompt to GPT-4: {prompt}")
        response = openai.Completion.create(
            engine="gpt-4",
            prompt=prompt,
            max_tokens=150,
            temperature=0.7
        )
        return response.choices[0].text.strip()
    except openai.error.OpenAIError as e:
        logging.error(f"API error occurred: {e}")
        return "An error occurred while processing your request."

# Test the function
response = debug_api_call("What's the weather like in Paris?")
print(response)
```

Explanation:

- This code snippet adds logging to monitor the API call and response.

- If the response is unexpected, you can inspect the log to identify whether the issue lies in the API call or the way data is being processed.

Best Practices for Debugging AI Apps:

- **Log and Monitor**: Log API calls and responses at different stages. This can help you trace the issue when things go wrong.

- **Use AI-specific Debugging Tools**: OpenAI offers a variety of error codes and logs that can help you understand API errors and limit issues.

- **Test for Edge Cases**: Make sure to test your application with various edge cases, such as ambiguous user inputs, unexpected queries, or requests that require long response times.

Ensuring Scalability and Reliability

For GPT-4-powered applications to be useful in production environments, they must be scalable and reliable. This section will focus on ensuring your application can handle varying loads, function correctly under stress, and remain stable over time.

Step 1: Implementing Load Balancing

Scalability is about ensuring your application can handle a large number of users simultaneously. One key technique for achieving scalability is load balancing, which distributes incoming requests across multiple servers or resources.

If your application relies heavily on GPT-4 API calls, you may want to consider the following approaches:

- **Rate Limiting**: Make sure your application handles API rate limits gracefully. Use retry logic and exponential backoff when the rate limit is reached.

- **Distributed Servers**: Deploy your application on multiple servers to distribute the load.

- **Caching**: Cache frequent responses to reduce the number of API calls. For example, responses to common queries like "What's the weather?" can be cached for a short period to avoid redundant API calls.

Example: Implementing Caching for Frequent Queries

To optimize API usage and reduce costs, you can implement caching for frequently asked questions.

```python
import time
import openai
import hashlib
from cachetools import TTLCache

# Set up OpenAI API key
openai.api_key = 'YOUR_OPENAI_API_KEY'

# Initialize a cache with a TTL of 60 seconds
cache = TTLCache(maxsize=100, ttl=60)

def get_cached_response(prompt):
    prompt_hash = hashlib.sha256(prompt.encode()).hexdigest()

    if prompt_hash in cache:
        return cache[prompt_hash]

    response = openai.Completion.create(
        engine="gpt-4",                    ↓
        prompt=prompt,
```

```
    response = openai.Completion.create(
        engine="gpt-4",
        prompt=prompt,
        max_tokens=150,
        temperature=0.7
    )
    answer = response.choices[0].text.strip()

    # Cache the response
    cache[prompt_hash] = answer
    return answer

# Example usage
prompt = "What's the weather like in New York?"
response = get_cached_response(prompt)
print(response)
```

Explanation:

- This code implements a caching mechanism to store the responses for frequent prompts.

- The TTLCache from the cachetools library caches responses for 60 seconds, reducing the need for repeated API calls for the same query.

Best Practices for Scalability:

- **Horizontal Scaling**: Consider scaling your infrastructure horizontally by adding more instances of your application when traffic increases.

- **Use Cloud Services**: Cloud platforms like AWS, Google Cloud, and Azure offer easy scaling and load-balancing options for handling fluctuating demands.

- **Optimize Database Calls**: Reduce unnecessary database queries by indexing important fields and caching frequently accessed data.

Step 2: Ensuring Reliability with Fault Tolerance

Reliability means that your application can continue functioning even when parts of it fail. This is especially important for AI-powered applications, as they depend on external services that can occasionally go down.

- **Graceful Degradation**: Design your app to degrade gracefully if the GPT-4 API is temporarily unavailable. Instead of crashing, the application should inform the user that the service is down and offer alternatives if possible.

- **Backup Data**: Regularly back up user data, logs, and other essential information to ensure you can recover quickly from failures.

Example: Handling API Failures Gracefully

```python
import openai
import time

openai.api_key = "YOUR_OPENAI_API_KEY"

def get_gpt_response(prompt):
    try:
        response = openai.Completion.create(
            engine="gpt-4",
            prompt=prompt,
            max_tokens=150,
            temperature=0.7
        )
        return response.choices[0].text.strip()
    except openai.error.OpenAIError:
        return "Sorry, the service is temporarily unavailable. Please try again later."

# Example usage
prompt = "What is the capital of Japan?"
response = get_gpt_response(prompt)
print(response)
```

Explanation:

- This example shows how to handle API errors and inform users when the service is down.

- The function retries the request, but if the error persists, it provides a fallback message.

Best Practices for Reliability:

- **Implement Retrying Logic**: Use retry strategies like exponential backoff to handle transient errors gracefully.

- **Monitor the Application**: Set up monitoring tools to track the health of the application and its dependencies in real-time.

- **Test Failures**: Regularly test failure scenarios to ensure your application can handle them effectively.

Optimizing for Speed, Cost, and User Experience

Optimizing GPT-4-powered applications involves making trade-offs between speed, cost, and user experience. While you want your application to be fast and responsive, you also need to keep costs in check, as frequent API calls can quickly become expensive.

Step 1: Reducing Latency

The speed of your application is critical for user experience. Latency refers to the delay between sending a request and receiving a response. Optimizing latency involves reducing the time it takes for your application to process a user's request.

- **Use Efficient Prompts**: Sending overly complex or verbose prompts can increase processing time. Make sure to keep prompts concise and clear.

- **Parallelize Requests**: If your application requires multiple GPT-4 calls (e.g., fetching data from multiple APIs), consider parallelizing the requests to reduce waiting time.

Step 2: Managing Costs

GPT-4 API usage can be costly, especially if your application involves large numbers of queries. Here are some strategies for cost optimization:

- **Optimize Token Usage**: Reduce the number of tokens in your prompts and responses to minimize the cost per API call.

- **Batch Processing**: For certain applications, you can process multiple requests in a batch to save costs.

Example: Cost Optimization Using Token Limits

```python
import openai

openai.api_key = 'YOUR_OPENAI_API_KEY'

def generate_optimized_response(prompt):
    response = openai.Completion.create(
        engine="gpt-4",
        prompt=prompt,
        max_tokens=100,  # Limit the response to 100 tokens
        temperature=0.7
    )
    return response.choices[0].text.strip()

# Example usage
prompt = "Tell me about the Eiffel Tower."
response = generate_optimized_response(prompt)
print(response)
```

Explanation:

- This example demonstrates how limiting the number of tokens in your response can help reduce the cost of each API call.

- Be mindful of the balance between brevity and informativeness.

Best Practices for Optimization:

- **Optimize API Calls**: Make only necessary API calls, and avoid redundancy.

- **Profile Performance**: Use profiling tools to measure how long your application takes to respond to users, and identify bottlenecks.

- **User-Centric Design**: Prioritize user experience by ensuring that the application is fast and easy to use.

Conclusion

Testing, debugging, and optimizing GPT-4-powered applications are crucial steps in ensuring that your app performs efficiently, is scalable, and delivers a positive user experience. By employing effective debugging techniques, optimizing for performance and cost, and ensuring scalability and reliability, you can build robust AI-powered tools that meet user expectations and scale with your application's growth.

www.ingramcontent.com/pod-product-compliance
Lightning Source LLC
Chambersburg PA
CBHW070210230526
45471CB00002B/906